THE TRUTH REGARDING BEING

BORN AGAIN

Convicted, Confronted, Transformed.

CHARLES O. SOYOYE

Published by New Generation Publishing in 2016

First Edition

www.newgeneration-publishing.com

New Generation Publishing

Being Born Again involves every area of our day-to-day life. Whatever you and I may have done in the past affects our life today. What we do today determines who we will be and what condition we find ourselves in tomorrow, next month and in the years to come. I believe that when you are obedient according to the Word of God, you will find fulfillment and peace even when faced with difficult situation.

DEDICATION

To my wife:

You are the most perfect and honest person I know. Your character is flawless and your motives always pure. You are a wonderful wife to me and a loving mother to our sons. I love you more now than ever before.

To my Sons:

You are my most treasured blessings. I love you all.

To my first child:

You are my first born and a remarkable son. You have made your mum and me very proud as you began your professional life. As you serve the Kingdom, God will continue to pour out blessings upon you and you will prosper all the days of your life in Jesus name. Amen.

I love you.

To my second child:

You are an awesome man of God, with a servant heart. With an anointing from above, your destiny in serving and loving God everyday is already beginning. Press more into the will and favour of God. He will bring to you everything you have asked of Him and much more.

I love you.

To my third child:

God is bringing good gifts into your life. He has a wonderful future planned for you. Follow Jesus intimately in all you do and you will prosper in all your ways. You are a good son, with the heart of a servant.

I love you.

REBIRTH

CONTENTS

THE TRUTH

Being a born again Christian is not a religion; it is a way of life to eternity in Christ Jesus. The truth is that religion can never save anyone but only the Lord Jesus Christ saves. Religion lead to violence, hatred among people and it is the brainchild of the devil. Religion aimed at confusing mankind concerning God's original plan and purpose to save through the Lord Jesus Christ from eternal perdition.

Hear what James, a servant of God and of the Lord Jesus Christ said about true religion, ***"External religious worship (religious as it is expressed in outward acts) that is pure and unblemished in the sight of God the Father is this; to visit and help and care for the orphans and widows in their affliction and need, and to keep oneself unspotted and uncontaminated from the world." (James 1:27.)***

God created the world and said that everyone that would come into it must be born of a woman. Stubbornly, mankind is experimenting different human creations, such as (test tube and designer babies) to play God. We call it human advancement to play God. Mankind has tried many other things contrary to the will and purpose of God but there is no way there.

Many people are now seeking to know God due to the world tumultuous situations, but are going through ways He has not recommend. Before anyone can see God, you must repent and accept the sacrifice of Jesus Christ. Paul and Silas answered the keeper of the prison, **"And they answered, *Believe on the Lord Jesus Christ (give yourself up to Him, take yourself out of your own keeping and entrust yourself into His keeping) and you will be saved, (and this applies both to) you and your household as well."* (Acts 16:31)**

There are many that say they are "**Christians**" that declare to believe in Jesus Christ as their Messiah, but there is little significant evidence from their life-decisions, attitudes, behaviours, convictions, conversations, morals, values, goals, habits that would reflect their lip service. If you really believe Jesus died for you and set you free from bondage to sin and spiritual death and if you really believe that the Creator of the Universe wants to have a personal, daily, intimate, and eternal relationship with you; your life should be radically, permanently, and consistently changing in every day life.

Actually, God has decreed the way man will enter His kingdom through His Son Jesus Christ. He is the only way to God according to the Scriptures. Thomas asks Jesus where He is going and how they can know the way. ***"Jesus said to him, I am the way and the Truth and the Life; no one comes to the Father except by (through) Me." (John 14:6.)*** Jesus gave them the answer to every destiny.

John the Apostle said, ***"In the beginning (before all time) was the Word (Christ), and the Word was with God, and the Word was God Himself. He was present originally with God. All things were made and came into existence through Him; and without Him was not even one thing made that has come into being. In Him was Life, and the Life was the Light of men. And the Light shines on in the darkness, for the darkness has never overpowered it (put it out or absorbed it or appropriated it, and is unreceptive to it). There came a man sent from God, whose name was John. This man came to witness, that he might testify of the Light, that all men might believe in it (adhere to it, trust it, and rely upon it) through him. He was not the Light himself, but came that he might bear witness regarding the Light.***

There it was-the true Light (was then) coming into the world (the genuine, perfect, steadfast Light) that illuminates every person. He came into the world, and though the world was made through Him, the world did not recognize Him (did not know Him). He came to that which belonged to Him (to His own-His domain, creation, things, world), and they who were His own did not receive Him and did not welcome Him. But to as

many as did receive and welcome Him, He gave the authority (power, privilege, right) to become the children of God, that is, to those who believe in (adhere to, trust in, and rely on) His name." (John 1:1-12).

Paul the Apostle said, *"(For I always pray to) the God of our Lord Jesus Christ, the Father of glory, that He may grant you a spirit of wisdom and revelation, (of insight into mysteries and secrets) in the (deep and intimate) knowledge of Him. By having the eyes of your heart flooded with light, so that you can know and understand the hope to which He has called you, and how rich is His glorious inheritance in the saints (His set-apart ones)." (Ephesians 1:17-18.)*

As the natural man hears the wind, so the man Born Again hears the voice of the Spirit. I am asking God to meet you at the point of your needs and manifest His Glory and His miracle working power regarding being Born Again in your life in Jesus name.

AMEN.

INTRODUCTION

The term "Being Born Again" is one of the most used phrases among present-day Christians. Yet, if asked what the term Being Born Again means, most church members could not give a clear explanation. The importance of this subject is shown in what Jesus said, "Except a man be Born Again, he cannot see the kingdom of God" (John 3:3). Jesus is saying that to be born again is to be saved. Being Born Again is the plan of salvation that Jesus authored at Calvary.

May I say that it is imperative that we understand what is required for us to be born again! All agree that when Jesus went to the cross, He brought in the means of salvation for everyone who will accept it. But what really happened at Calvary? What can it do for me? How do I accept what was done there in my own personal life?

I believe that when Jesus went to the cross, He brought in the means of salvation for everyone who will accept it. But what really happened at Calvary is the reason why this book is written just for you to know what can it do for you. So that you can accept what was done there at Calvary in your own personal life that Jesus Christ is your Lord and Saviour.

At Calvary, there were three steps to the work of Christ; death, burial, and resurrection (I Corinthians 15:1-4). It is very easy to see that these three steps make up the act of Being Born Again spoken of by Jesus Christ in (John 3:1-5); to die, to be buried, and to rise again. (That is to be Born Again). So we see that Jesus, through His death, burial, and resurrection, bought for us the plan of Being Born Again spoken of in (John 3:3), whereby we receive salvation.

The truth I want you to understand is that Jesus purchased a plan of salvation for you and me is the greatest news the world has ever received. The thing you must understand is that not only was it necessary for Jesus to do something, but also it is absolutely essential for us to act upon what He did.

Hear what Jesus told Nicodemus, "You must be born again" (John 3:7). Now the astonishing thing is that Nicodemus was a religious leader of his day; yet, he had no concept of what it meant to be Born Again! We find that the very same thing is true in the day in which we live. Many men and women who fill positions of spiritual leadership in our world have no real understanding of the Born Again experience. Nicodemus inquired of Jesus in John 3:4, "How can a man be born when he is old? can he enter the second time into his mother's womb, and be born?"

Jesus answered, "Verily, verily, I say unto thee, Except a man be born of water and of the Spirit, he cannot enter into the kingdom of God." You can't be born again of a woman. The second birth is a spiritual birth. Notice that Jesus said without being Born Again we cannot see or enter the kingdom of God. In other words, we cannot be saved.

Hear what the Bible say that happened on the day of Pentecost when Peter preached the first message after Calvary, the men cried out, "What must we do?" "Then Peter said unto them, Repent, and be baptized every one of you in the name of Jesus Christ for the remission of sins and ye shall receive the gift of the Holy Ghost" (Acts 2:38). Peter was giving them the plan of salvation, REPENTANCE, BAPTISM, The infilling of the HOLY GHOST.If being born again is to be saved, Peter was evidently talking to them about being saved.

The reality regarding being **Born Again** is to undergo a "**Spiritual Rebirth**" (regeneration) the human soul or spirit, contrasted with the physical birth everyone experiences. The Bible mentions that, "***As Jesus talked with Nicodemus, He said, "I tell you the truth, no one can see the kingdom of God unless he is born again. How can a man be born when he is old? Nicodemus asked. 'Surely he cannot enter a second time into his***

mother's womb to be born!' Jesus answered, 'I tell you the truth, no one can enter the kingdom of God unless he is born of water and the Spirit. Flesh gives birth to flesh, but the Spirit gives birth to spirit. You should not be surprised at my saying, 'You must be born again" (John 3:3-7.)

To be born again is connected with salvation in Christ Jesus. Anyone who professes to be born again must have a personal relationship with the Lord Jesus Christ, the son of the living God. That means that you are connected with salvation by accepting Jesus Christ as your Lord and Saviour. Anyone who acknowledges to be born again must have a personal relationship with the Lord Jesus Christ. It literally means there must be a transformation from God and a renewal in righteousness and true holiness to be saved.

The phrase to be born again is literally means "**born from above**." Nicodemus had a real need like you and I. He needed a change of his heart, that is, a spiritual transformation. (**John 3:3-7.**) New birth, being born again, is an act of God whereby eternal life is imparted to the person who believes. (**2 Corinthians 5:17.) (Titus 3:5.) (1 Peter 1:3.) (1 John 2:29. 3:9. 4:7. 5:1-4. 18.**) The Bible indicates that "***born again***" also carries the idea "***to become children of God***" ***(John 1:12, 13.***) through trust in the name of the Lord Jesus Christ.

The reason of writing this book is to let you understand the reason why you must truly be born again and not just attending church alone. The truth you must understand is that attending church services alone without accepting the Lord Jesus Christ as your Lord and Saviour cannot and will not help you see the kingdom of God. The Apostle Paul said, "***And you He made alive, who were dead in trespasses and sins...***" ***(Ephesians 2:1.***) To the Romans, Paul wrote, "***For all have sinned and fall short of the glory of God.***" ***(Romans 3:23.***) So, you need to be born again in order to have your sins forgiven and have a relationship with God. Church attendance alone without accepting the Lord Jesus Christ as your Lord and Saviour cannot and will not take you to heaven.

How does one come to have a relationship with God? The Bible say "***For it is by grace you have been saved, through faith—and this not from yourselves, it is the gift of God—not by works, so that no one can boast***." ***(Ephesians 2:8-9***.) When one is "save," he/she has been born again, spiritually renewed, and is now a child of God by right of new birth. Trusting, accepting and believing in the Lord Jesus Christ, the One who paid the penalty of sin when He die on the cross is what it means to be "Born ***Again***" spiritually. "***Therefore, if anyone is in Christ, he is a new creation: the old has gone, the new has come***!" (***2 Corinthians 5:17***.)

There is a fundamental law that you must understand both in the natural and spiritual realm that we live. It is either you live after the flesh or after the Spirit. The truth is that it is God's will that all men be save and begotten by His Word of Truth. For the Word of Truth is one of the agent that make a born again child of God new creature! It is by His Word of Truth that you are inborn and implanted in the soul that one is saved and begotten. The Word of God is the seed and when it is implanted in the soul, it germinates and spring forth into eternal life. Only the seed that fail to be sown on properly prepared soil, and cared for, will fail to bring forth fruit.

"***For the Word of God is living and active. Sharper than any double-edged sword, it penetrates even to dividing soul and spirit, joints and marrow; it judges the thoughts and attitudes of the heart***." (***Hebrews 4:12***.) In reality, many people deny the authority of the Word of God, (the Bible) because they do not want God telling them what to do. But for those who are willing to know the truth, it is very clear. God alone can foretell the future and then bring it to pass. These stand as an irrefutable proof of His existence and of the divine origin of the Bible for those willing to look into it, accept it and believe Him.

That is why Prophet Isaiah was commanded by God to

make announcement to the Gentiles to bring them near so they could declare their strongest arguments regarding why they worshipped and trusted in lifeless gods that could not save. "***Who foretold this long ago, who declared it from the distant past? Was it not I, the LORD? And there is no God apart from me, a righteous God and a Saviour; there is none but me. Turn to me and be saved, all you ends of the earth; for I am God, and there is no other.***" (***Isaiah 45:21-22***.) God challenged comparison of other gods with Himself, and again He declared Himself the only true and living God.

If you have never trust in the Lord Jesus Christ as your Lord and Savior! Will you consider the prompting of the Holy Spirit as He speaks to your heart right now? You must be born again. "***Yet to all who received him, to those who believed in his name, he gave the right to become children of God— children born not of natural descent, nor of human decision or a husband's will, but born of God***" (***John 1:12-13***.) Here is a sample prayer! Remember that saying this prayer or any other prayer will not save you. It is only trusting in Christ Jesus that can save you. This prayer is the simply way to express to God your faith in Him and thank Him for provision for your salvation.

The Reason to be Born Again

The Bible teaches that to be born again means to turn away from sin and rebellion against Christ and receive God nature, and then live a life of holiness. Jesus told Nicodemus he needed to be "***born agai***n" before he could see the kingdom of God. (***John 3:3.)*** Before the new birth, Jesus said, people's unbelief and sin condemns them to hell, and they need to be "***saved.***" God's Spirit convinces a person that he or she is a sinner in need of God's forgiveness, and many times the Spirit of God confronts a person who is blatantly sinning. ***(John 3:16-20.)***

The Apostle Paul was converted on the Road to Damascus, an experience he received as "***regeneration.***" (**Acts 9) (Titus 3:5**.) "***Therefore if any person is (in grafted) in Christ (the Messiah) he is a new creature (a new creature altogether), the old (previous moral and spiritual condition) has passed away. Behold the fresh and new has come!" (2 Corinthians 5:17.)*** This is the Spirit and nature of God in renewed man. The new nature must be put on and it must manifest righteousness and true holiness after repenting and believing. Then a life of holiness and righteousness begins through the power of God. (***Ephesians 4:24.)***

Born-again Christians ought to stop doing the things that characterized their former life. Behaviours listed including lying, stealing, greed, foul language and fornication must be eradicated. (**Ephesians 4:25**.) It is the lie and all other things of your former life that must be put away. This has to do with putting away Satan who is the father of all lies. These days, it is a common thing for the heathen teacher to declare that a lie is better than the truth when it is profitable and less hurtful. These things bring God's wrath on lost people. Having been brought up in such loose system of morality, any new convert need this warning.

For that reason, true Christians should not continued in

such activities. Instead, they should, ***"(Live) as children of obedience (to God); do not conform yourselves to the evil desires (that govern you) in your former ignorance (when you did not know the requirement of the Gospel)."*** **(1 Peter 1:14.)** According to Paul, he said, instead of lying, Christians should speak the truth; instead of stealing, Christians should work. (***Ephesians: 4***.) Christians should be kind instead of evil speaking, tenderhearted and forgiving. Paul wrote that fornicators, covetous people and idolaters had "***no inheritance in the kingdom of Christ and God***." (***Ephesians 5:5.)*** In addition, people should not be drunk with wine, but should be filled with the Spirit. (***Ephesians 5:18.***)

Convicted, Confronted, Converted

Jesus said that when the Holy Spirit have comes, He would condemn the world of sin because the people do not believe in Jesus Christ and His righteousness, (***John 16:8-11.)*** Therefore, when the Holy Spirit arrived on the Day of Pentecost, (***Acts 2:1-4***), God could fill multitudes with the Holy Spirit and empower them to reflect the righteousness of Christ when he walked on the earth. Born-again Christians ought to stop doing the things that characterize their former life such behaviours as lying, stealing, greed, foul language and fornication. Paul writes that these things bring God's wrath on lost people. ***(Ephesians 4:22-25.)***

Behaviour Changes Demonstrate The New Nature

The truth that change brings about by the **New Birth** should alert others that something has happened in a person's life. Often the emphasis of teacher and preachers is placed on "**telling others about Jesus**" apart from demonstrating that one's life is different. The most powerful way of witnessing is the example you set by the way you live your life according to God's way. If you are a true born again Christian, you will not be able to hide your faith indefinitely despite doing your good works with as little fuss as possible. Questions about your faith and belief will unavoidably arise. I believe that your good example as a married person often prove a far more effective persuader to those who are married.

Humanly speaking, your spouse is probably the most important person in your Christian life. Your life partner also becomes the number one neighbour you should love. So you have to be more careful how you speak within the husband and wife relationship, especially if your spouse is an unbeliever. I can understand that trying to persuade an unbelieving husband or wife to follow the main values of the Christian faith can prove a perilous task.

The apostle Peter advocates a right approach, "***In like manner, you married women, be submissive to your own husbands (subordinate yourselves as being secondary to and dependent on them, and adapt yourselves to them), so that even if any do not obey the Word (of God) they may be won over not by discussion but by the (godly) lives of their wives." (1 Peter 3:1.***) Your good examples often prove a far more effective persuader than your good words and fair speeches. "***Husbands likewise, (should) dwell with them with understanding (or knowledge), giving honour to the wife……" (1 Peter 3:7.)***

Although many non-Christians tend to think of new Christians as having decided to make changes in their life, the new birth is not the result of "turning over a new leaf," or "will power." Changes brought about by the work of the Spirit of God take place inside a person in the supernatural operation that accompanies repentance and the new birth. One must be born "**of the Spirit**," Jesus said, "***What is born of (from) the flesh is flesh (of the physical is physical); and what is born of the Spirit is spirit." (John 3:6.)***

Being Born Again Is A Supernatural Act That Brings Change

The Bible teaches that changes in the lives of Christians are not a matter of self-effort. **Being Born Again** involves three acts of the Spirit of God: ***Convincing*** individuals of their sinfulness, ***Confronting*** them and ***Converting*** them from godlessness to relationship as God's children. When a person is converted from sin to righteousness, changes should be evident in the person's life. Born again Christians should be kind, tenderhearted and forgiving, not fornicators, envious, idolaters or drunkards.

What does Jesus mean that we must be Born of Water and of Spirit?

Let's read the whole conversation to get the teaching of what Jesus said to Nicodemus for the Bible say, ***"There was a man of the Pharisees named Nicodemus, a ruler of the Jews. This man came to Jesus by night and said to Him, "Rabbi, we know that You are a teacher come from God; for no one can do these signs that You do unless God is with him." Jesus answered and said to him, "Most assuredly, I say to you, unless one is born again, he cannot see the kingdom of God." Nicodemus said to Him, "How can a man be born when he is old? Can he enter a second time into his mother's womb and be born?" Jesus answered, "Most assuredly, I say to you, unless one is born of water and the Spirit, he cannot enter the kingdom of God. "That which is born of the flesh is flesh, and that which is born of the Spirit is spirit". Do not marvel that I said to you, you must be born again.***

"The wind blows where it wishes, and you hear the sound of it, but cannot tell where it comes from and where it goes. So is everyone who is born of the Spirit." Nicodemus answered and said to Him, How can these things be? Jesus answered and said to him, "Are you the teacher of Israel, and do not know these things?" Most assuredly, I say to you, we speak what we know and testify what we have seen, and you do not receive our witness. "If I have told you earthly things and you do not believe, how will you believe if I tell you heavenly things? No one has ascended to heaven but He who came down from heaven, that is, the Son of Man who is in heaven."(John 3:1-13.)

Jesus is having a conversation with Nicodemus, who was a Pharisee. Jesus spoke to Nicodemus in accordance to the Pharisee's teaching- to be born of water meant to be born physically. This is proved by Nicodemus remark who thought to be born again meant a physical birth ***"How can***

a man be born when he is old? Can he enter a second time into his mother's womb and be born*?* Jesus proceeds to say, "***Unless one is born of water and the Spirit, you cannot enter the kingdom of God.***" Nicodemus, who was a Pharisee, believed like the other Jews that because he was born a Jew and kept God's ordinances that he should automatically enter into the kingdom of God. However, Jesus explains this is not enough.

Jesus interpret the water as flesh (a physical birth) "***That which is born of the flesh is flesh, and that which is born of the Spirit is spirit.***" He says of being born of water is to be born of the flesh. Jesus explains the difference, telling Nicodemus you have already had a physical birth, you are in need of another birth "***Do not marvel that I said to you, "You must be born again.***" Literally from the Spirit above is to enter the kingdom of God. You must be born again ***"that which is born of the Spirit is spirit."*** The new birth from above is a second birth which gives us eternal life. The new birth is invisible; he likens it to the wind. It is not from the water beneath (***the flesh***) but of the Spirit (literally, in the Greek, **from above)**. He is contrasting the natural ***(flesh)*** to the spiritual (***Spirit***).

There is always a distinction between water and Spirit baptism. Scripture tells us that John came baptizing with water and he said, ***"There is one who will come after me. . . He will baptize you with the Holy Spirit" (Mk. 1:7-8; Mt. 3:11; Jn. 1:33).*** The flesh and the spirit are two different properties; two different things. So there are two births- one of the flesh and the other of the spirit that comes from God. ***"That which is born of the flesh is flesh, and that which is born of the Spirit is spirit. Do not marvel that I said to you, you must be born again" (John 3:6-7.)***

"Beloved, let us love one another, for love is of God; and everyone who loves is born of God and knows God" (I John 4:7.) This is the love of God shed in a believer's heart by believing the gospel.

"Whoever believes that Jesus is the Christ is born of God, and everyone who loves Him who begot also loves him *who is begotten of Him.*" (I John 5:1.) These unquestionably have everything to do with the gospel of Christ Jesus.

"For whatever is born of God overcomes the world. And this is the victory that has overcome the world-- our faith." (I John 5:4.) The new nature of the spirit of God has our affections change toward God and not toward the fallen world.

"Whoever has been born of God does not sin, for His seed remains in him; and he cannot sin, because he has been born of God." (I John 3:9.)

"We know that whoever is born of God does not sin; but he who has been born of God keeps himself, and the wicked one does not touch him." (I John 5:18.) There is life change where one lives more in righteousness than they do in the old way of life in sin. John explains that, ***"If you know that He is righteous, you know that everyone who practices righteousness is born of Him" (I John 2:29.)***

"But now we have been delivered from the law, having died to what we were held by, so that we should serve in the newness of the Spirit and not in the oldness of the letter." (Romans 7:6.)

Chapter 1

SPIRITUAL REBIRTH

Spiritual Rebirth is a time at which the regenerative power of the Spirit of God comes into a person's heart and gives new birth to their spirit with the seed of the Word of God. The Bible say, ***"You have been regenerated (born again), not from a mortal origin (seed, sperm), but from one that is immortal by the ever living and lasting Word of God."*** (1 ***Peter 1:23.)*** The new birth by the Word of God!

In the Garden of Eden, Adam and Eve walked with God. They had spiritual union with God until their fall. God said that in the day they ate of the tree of the knowledge of good and evil, they would die. The Lord God said, ***"But of the tree of the knowledge of good and evil and blessing and calamity you shall not eat, for in the day that you eat of it you shall surely die." (Genesis 2:17.)***

All the same, in their natural lives, they lived on for several hundred years. The Bible indicates that it was a spiritual death. ***"Then the eyes of them both were opened, and they knew that they were naked; and they sewed fig leaves together and made themselves apron like girdles." (Genesis 3:7.)***

Adam and Eve lost God-consciousness and gained self-consciousness. They lost the power to do the good, and gained the power to do evil. Thus, instead of becoming like God, they became unlike Him, in that He has the power to do only good. It is morally impossible for God to sin. Adam and Even lost that glorious sinless and innocent-looking countenance comparable to that of Elohim.

When the spirit of man died, it cut off spiritual union with God. Jesus said, ***"God is a Spirit (a spiritual Being) and those who worship Him must worship Him in spirit***

and in truth (reality).” (***John 4:24.)*** Let me emphasize this clearly that God is a Spirit Being, not the sun, moon, stars, nor any image of wood, stone or metal and not beast or man.

Adam and Eve were judged by God and driven out of the garden. As for the consequence, spiritual death passed unto all mankind according to (Genesis 3). Apostle Paul said, “***Therefore, as sin came into the world through one man, and death as the result of sin, so death spread to all men, (no one being able to stop it or to escape its power) because all men sinned.” (Romans 5:12.)*** Death did not come by personal sin, as it did in the case of Adam. Death passed upon all men because of Adam’s sin. (Genesis 2:17; Romans 5:12-21).

The Bible says that ***“Now the promises (covenants, agreements) were decreed and made to Abraham and his Seed (this Offspring, his heir). He (God) does not say, And to seeds (descendants, heirs), as if referring to many persons, but, and to your Seed (your Descendant, your Heir), obviously referring to one individual, who is (none other than) Christ (the Messiah).” (Galatians 3:16.)***

Jesus Christ is the last Adam. “***And so it is written. The first man Adam was made a living soul; the last Adam was made a quickening spirit.” (1 Corinthians*** 1***5:45.)*** The last Adam (Jesus Christ) was made a quickening spirit, who is the necessity of resurrection.

There is a natural enmity between snakes and men, as well as between children of Satan and God because of the curse on Satan. God said, “***And I will put enmity between thee and the woman, and between thy seed and her seed; it shall bruise thy head, and thou shall bruise his heel.” (Genesis 3:15.)***

The serpent being Satan, deceived man to fall. The seed of the woman is a reference to the Lord Jesus Christ. He was sent from God the Father. Jesus said, ***“For God so loved the world that he gave his only begotten Son, that whosoever believeth in him should not perish, but have everlasting life.” (John 3:16.)***

Jesus Christ came to the earth to give His life a ransom for the sins of the world and reverse the Adamic curse. ***"For if by one man's offence death reigned by one; much more they which receive abundance of grace and of the gift of righteousness shall reign in life by one, Jesus Christ," (Romans 5:17.)***

The truth is that through Adam's sin, a sentence of death, without a promise of resurrection, passed upon all men; so, by the obedience of Christ Jesus taking man's place, the sentence was completely canceled and original dominion restored. One is constituted a sinner through Adam, not by his personal sins, so one is constituted righteous through Christ, not by his personal acts of righteousness.

Jesus Christ is the only mediator between God and man, for the Bible say, "***For there (is only) one God, and (only) one Mediator between God and men, the man Christ Jesus. Who gave Himself a ransom for all (people, a fact that was) attested to at the right and proper time," (1Timothy 2:5-6.)*** These signify a ransom paid for the redemption of a captive, and an exchange of one person for another or the redemption of life for life.

Chapter 2

BEING BORN AGAIN

The regenerative power of the Holy Spirit complete the born again experience when one accept Jesus Christ as his Lord and Saviour. When a person believes in his or her heart that God raised Jesus from the dead and confess with his or her mouth that He is The Lord! This is how to receive God's righteousness by the word of faith, and if acted upon, you shall be saved.

Apostle Paul said, ***"Because if you acknowledge and confess with your lips that Jesus is Lord and in your heart believe (adhere to, trust in, and rely on the truth) that God raised Him from the dead, you will be saved. For with the heart a person believes (adhere to, trust in, and relies on Christ) and so is justified (declared righteous, according to God), and with the mouth he confesses (declares openly and speaks out freely his faith) and confirms (his) salvation."*** (***Romans 10:9-10.)***

Eternal life is a free gift, ***"For the wages which sin pays is death, but the (bountiful) free gift of God is eternal life through (in union with) Jesus Christ our Lord,"*** (***Romans 6:23.)*** When you accept the shed blood of Christ for your sins and put your faith or trust in the blood, then you will receive the free gift of God that is waiting for you, that is "***eternal life***".

The truth is that God have set forth, made, appointed, and published this sacrifice to be propitiation, or covering for sin. This is the act of God whereby He becomes gracious to the sinner through Jesus Christ. ***"Whom God hath set forth to be a propitiation through faith in his blood, to declare his righteousness for the remission of sins that are past, through the forbearance of God,"*** (***Romans 3:25.)***

You too can be made clean and whole, washed

completely of all sin. If you come to the light and expose yourself and allow God to bring resurrection life to you then you can become the new creature that God has made you, on the inside. Scriptures teach that life is in the blood, and in the blood of Christ is His very life. This is a scientific fact as well, when we consider that ones make-up and everything they are in the natural is contained in the DNA of their blood cells.

Eating and drinking is used figuratively of partaking of the benefit of the death of Christ. Eating of Christ simply means that man must accept by faith what Christ did for him and live by obedience to Him without sin so the penalty of sin will not have to be paid again. ***"And Jesus said to them, I assure you, most solemnly I tell you, you cannot have any life in you unless you eat the flesh of the Son of Man and drink His blood (unless you appropriate His life and the saving merit of His blood)." (John 6:53.)***

You are cleansed from all sins from the time of confession and God will be faithful, just, forgive and cleanse you from all unrighteousness. ***"If we (freely) admit that we have sinned and confess our sins, He is faithful and just (true to His own nature and promises) and will forgive our sins (dismiss our lawlessness) and (continuously) cleanse us from all unrighteousness (everything not in conformity to His will in purpose, thought, and action)." (1 John 1:9.)***

However if one does fall into sin he still has hope and can confess sin and be cleansed again. This makes a way for God to come into a person's heart and regenerate their spirit. For God is a Holy God and cannot dwell in sin. Therefore, Jesus Christ makes a way for the sinner to become born again.

Jesus is talking to Nicodemus and says that, ***"Marvel not (do not be surprised, astonished) at my telling you. You must all be born anew (from above)." (John 3:7.)*** If Jesus said that we must be born again, then we must be born again, ***"Jesus answered and said unto him, Verily, verily, I say unto thee, Except a man be born again, he***

cannot see the kingdom of God," (John 3:3.)

Once more, ***"Jesus answered, I assured you, most solemnly I tell you, unless a man is born of water and (even) the Spirit, he cannot (ever) enter the kingdom of God." (John 3:5.)*** As the natural man hears the wind, so the man born again hears the voice of the Spirit. The phrase **born again** comes from two Greek words, **gennao** and **anothen,** meaning **born from above**.

As soon as a man or woman accept the shed blood of Christ and the fact that Jesus Christ gave His life for their life and they believe that He saved them, the moment they release their faith in this fact, the Spirit of God comes into their heart and makes them born from above.

Both outward and inward sin must pass away or one cannot claim to be in Christ. Old things are passed away and all things become new. ***"Therefore if any person is (in grafted) in Christ (the Messiah) he is a new creation (a new creature altogether); the old (previous moral and spiritual condition) has passed away. Behold the fresh and new has come." (2 Corinthians 5:17.)***

The assumption that only outward transgressions are forgiven and one is still under control of the old man, the devil, is one of the most erroneous doctrines in Christendom. Once one has been regenerate, by the incorruptible seed of the Word of God through the operation of the Holy Spirit, they become a new creation in Christ and as we have indicated, ***"old things are passed away and all things have become new."*** The tense of that scripture says it all – **have become new**.

It is up to us to begin to have a good acknowledgment of faith in the fact that we are now new creations in Christ and not be moved by that which we see in our lives that would contradict what we would think would be Christ-like. Peter wrote about divine nature. The result of being born again is the fact that we no longer have to try to become Christ-like through outward rules of the old law, but through a new covenant with God.

Apostle Paul said, ***"(And I pray) that the participation***

in and sharing of your faith may produce and promote full recognition and appreciation and understanding and precise knowledge of every good (thing) that is ours in (our identification with) Christ Jesus (and unto His glory)." (Philemon 1:6.)

We have been made partakers of divine nature of the growth of true knowledge. ***"By means of these He has bestowed on us His precious and exceedingly great promises, so that through them you may escape (by flight) from the moral decay (rottenness and corruption) that is in the world because of covetousness (lust and greed), and become shares (partakers) of the divine nature."(2 Peter 1:4.)***

And even as we were sinners by natural world or that is to say, failures, missing the mark, and no one had to teach us how to sin, even so, by a new and living way, we can walk in the originality of life as normal and easy as one would breathe the air.

Chapter 3

WATER BAPTISM

We are command by Christ to be baptized in water. "***He that believeth and is baptized shall be saved; but he that believeth not shall be damned." (Mark 16:16.)*** Water baptism is an outward profession of faith, "***The like figure whereunto even baptism doth also now save us (not the putting away of the filth of the flesh, but the answer of a good conscience toward God) by the resurrection of Jesus Christ.*" *(1 Peter 3:21.)***

Consequently, in these scripture it is a confession of your inward death, burial and resurrection in Christ. In it, we are portraying the fact that Jesus Christ took our sins upon Him and in Him we were crucified. In Him we died and in Him we are resurrected to walk in the newness of life. "***We were buried therefore with Him by the baptism into death, so that just as Christ was raised from the dead by the glorious (power) of the Father, so we too might (habitually) live and behave in newness of life." (Romans 6:4.)***

It is through this sacrament that our faith is fortified and completely released. It has no other significance other than that it portrays the actual experience of being born again and baptized by the Spirit of God into the death, burial, and resurrection of Jesus Christ, "***For by one Spirit are we all baptized into one body, whether we be Jews or Gentiles, whether we be bond or free; and have been all made to drink into one Spirit," (1 Corinthians 12:13.)*** with an operation not made by human hands.

"***In whom also ye are circumcised with the circumcision made without hands, in putting off the body of the sins of the flesh by the circumcision of Christ: Buried with him in baptism, wherein also ye are risen with him through the faith of the operation of God, who***

hath raised him from the dead. And you, being dead in your sins and the uncircumcision of your flesh, hath he quickened together with him, having forgiven you all trespasses; Blotting out the handwriting of ordinances that was against us, which was contrary to us, and took it out of the way, nailing it to his cross; And having spoiled principalities and powers, he made a show of them openly, triumphing over them in it." (Colossians 2:11-15.)

The word baptism in the New Testament comes from the Greek word baptizo and it means to dip or immerse. Total emersion is the proper New Testament procedure for baptism after one believes. Jesus said, ***"He who believes (who adheres to and trusts in and relies on the Gospel and Him whom it sets forth) and is baptized will be saved (from the penalty of eternal death); but he who does not believe (who does not adhere to and trust in and rely on the Gospel and Him whom it sets forth) will be condemned." (Mark 16:16.)***

These symbolize being buried with Christ in His death. In essence, we are saying we believe the old man of sin is dead and we are going to walk a new walk of victory through the resurrection power of the Holy Spirit.

BORN TWICE

The Bible said that we must be born of water and of spirit. ***"Jesus answered, Verily, verily, I say unto thee, except a man be born of water and of the Spirit, he cannot enter into the kingdom of God." (John 3:5.)*** In other word, once you've been born naturally by water, then you must be born spiritually in order to see and enter into the Kingdom of God.

At the end of this natural life, every human being will face life or death in eternity. Eternal life or eternal death! If you are born twice, you will die once, meaning you will have natural death and then eternal life. If you are born once, you will die twice. You experience natural death and then have to face eternal death.

"And the sea gave up the dead who were in it; and death and hell delivered up the dead who were in them: and they were judged every man according to their works. And death and hell were cast into the lake of fire. This is the second death. And whosoever was not found written in the book of life was cast into the lake of fire." (Revelation 20:13-15.)

Chapter 4

ACCEPTING JESUS CHRIST

If you have not acknowledged Jesus Christ as your Lord and Saviour by asking Him into your heart through the person of the Holy Spirit, it would be wise on your part to do so upon the reading of this book. This is done by confessing with your mouth that He is Lord and believing in your heart that He was raised from the dead.

For you to receive the righteousness of God, the Bible said, ***"That if thou shall confess with thy mouth the Lord Jesus, and shall believe in your heart that God hath raised him from the dead, thou shall be saved for with the heart man believeth unto righteousness; and with the mouth confession is made unto salvation."*** (***Romans 10:9-10.)*** It is the word of faith, and if acted upon, you shall be saved. This is a simple guarantee of salvation.

SIMPLY PRAY THIS PRAYER FROM YOUR HEART:

Father in heaven, I know that I have sinned and need forgiveness. I offer you my life and ask for cleansing through the blood of Jesus Christ. I confess Jesus Christ as Lord and I believe in my heart that He willingly died for my sins and was raise from the dead on the third day. Holy Spirit, I ask you to come into my heart and make me transform from God and a renewal in righteousness and true holiness to be saved. Thank you Father for doing this through the person of the Holy Spirit, In Jesus name. Amen.

MAINTAING YOUR WORK

If you are to purchase a new car, you would find within the confines of the car's handbook, a maintenance plan designed to keep the vehicle at an optimum performance level. Likewise, there is a simple maintenance plan that can be found within the handbook of life (God's word). The maintenance plan of which I am referring to is a plan that has been designed to maintain your right relationship with God and the body of Christ.

It is also designed to keep you at a level of clear awareness to produce a steady supply of hope, joy, peace and prosperity that the world cannot give, nor take away. Jesus said, ***"Peace I leave with you; my (own) peace I now give and bequeath to you. Not as the world gives do I give to you. Do not let your hearts be troubled, neither let them be afraid. (Stop allowing yourselves to be agitated and disturbed; and do not permit yourselves to be fearful and intimidated and cowardly and unsettled)." (John 14:27.)***

THE MAINTENANCE PLANS

(A.) **Get into a local, Spirit-filled Word church:**

The Bible says, ***"And when the day of Pentecost was fully come, they were all with one accord in one place. And suddenly there came a sound from heaven as of a rushing mighty wind, and it filled the entire house where they were sitting. And there appeared unto them cloven tongues like as of fire, and it sat upon each of them. And they were all filled with the Holy Ghost, and began to speak with other tongues, as the Spirit gave them utterance." (Acts 2:1-4.)***

It doesn't have to be glorious in the external sense. It does not have to have a huge number of members, but it should be a place where, within your heart, you sense God would have you to be. You could even be meeting with believers in someone's home. A place wherein its members have a heart and longing for the return of the Lord Jesus Christ and display fervency of spirit in prayer and the study of the Word of God.

There are so many influences today by peers in the world to entice and meeting with a good fellowship of believers on a regular weekly basis will counter the influence of people around us who would rather serve this world's system. ***"You (are like) unfaithful wives (having illicit love affairs with the world and breaking your marriage vow to God)' do you not know that being the world's friend is being God's enemy? So whoever chooses to be a friend of the world takes his stand as an enemy of God." (James 4:4.)***

Think for example, a cluster of charcoals. When lit and packed closely, they burn with fervent heat. If you were to separate one from the rest, all alone, its fire would soon diminish and die. The fire of the believer is likewise. Jesus said, ***"For wherever two or three are gathered (drawn together as my followers) in (into) my name, there I AM in the midst of them." (Matthew 18:20.)***

Consider also a flock of sheep grazing. The wolf (devil) shyly observes from the hillside, waiting to see which one will separate itself from the rest of the flock and make his job easy. If none do through self will and self assurance, he is likely to attempt to divide and separate the sheep (scatter them) so as to capture one of them!

Remember well the admonition of the Apostle Paul not to forsake the assembling of you together. ***"Not forsaking or neglecting to assemble together (as believers), as is the habit of some people, but admonishing (warning, urging, and encouraging) one another, and all the more faithfully as you see the day approaching." (Hebrews 10:25.)*** These is our duty to one another as a believer and be regular church attendant.

(B.) A daily devotional time:

It is very important that the Christian be armed with prayer on a daily basis. ***"Pray at all times (on every occasion, in every season) in the Spirit, with all (manner of) prayer and entreaty. To that end keep alert and watch with***

strong purpose and perseverance, interceding in behalf of all the saints (God's consecrated people)." (Ephesians 6:18,) This is every believer's resource.

May I encourage you to begin your day with a time of prayer, meditative thought and scripture reading? This helps to awaken the spirit and set straight the day's path. It does not have to be a long, ritualistic procedure with the thought of pleasing God in doing so, but rather consistency is the key, accompanied by the awareness that you are keeping yourself in tune with the Holy Spirit.

The truth is that a portion of time for prayer concerning the matters of the day, a portion of time for scripture reading and a portion of time for meditative thought may be accomplished in anywhere from five minutes to a half-hour's time. The results will last an entire day. Praying is not classed as part of the armour, but is an additional and very important part of the fight against spiritual powers of evil.

You have to be prudent to repeat this procedure at mid-day and especially prior to retiring for the night. "***Now when Daniel knew that the writing was signed, he went into his house; and his windows being open in his chamber toward Jerusalem, he kneeled upon his knees three times a day, and prayed, and gave thanks before his God, as he did aforetime***." ***(Daniel 6:10.)***

Think about it to be to your spirit what showering, washing your hair and brushing your teeth are to your body. How much more important to you is your eternal spirit in comparison with your temporal body? Your spirit is the candle of the Lord. "***The spirit of man is the candle of the Lord, searching all the inward parts of the belly.***" ***(Proverbs 20:27.)*** God uses the spirit of man as a light to search out the inward parts and determine what is good or bad.

When you learn to keep it, it will pervade all dimensions of living with its powerful, positive influence. A devotional time should also be conducted collectively with brothers and sisters in the body of Christ. "***These all***

***continued with one accord in prayer and supplication, with the women, and Mary the mother of Jesus, and with his brethren.*" *(Act 1:14)*. When it is practiced with our family and friends in the church, it will fill many needs that are otherwise filled with an overdose of secular activity.

(C.) **Speaking and thinking good things:**

How to live in Christian virtues, Paul said, ***"Finally, brethren, whatsoever things are true, whatsoever things are honest, whatsoever things are just, whatsoever things are pure, whatsoever things are lovely, and whatsoever things are of good report: if there be any virtue, and if there be any praise, think on these things. Those things, which ye have both learned, and received, and heard, and seen in me, do: and the God of peace shall be with you." (Philippians 4:8-9.)***

The truth is that not only are Christians to meditate on certain things but they are to do certain things. Christianity is very practical. It is not a dead, dry, formal, human religion of rituals, outward form, and show, but a divine, living, vital, dynamic, liberating religion. I believe that one without power to deliver you and I from sin sickness, poverty, and want, now and hereafter, is not of God.

Filthy communications corrupt good manners. ***"Strip yourselves of your former nature [put off and discard your old unrenowned self] which characterized your previous manner of life and becomes corrupt through lusts and desires that spring from delusion." (Ephesians 4:22.)*** The things we say and think are going to effect the way we and others around us believe and in order for the believer to nurture their faith, a profession or confession of faith will have to be practiced.

"Let us hold fast the profession of our faith without wavering; for he is faithful that promised."(Hebrews 10:23.) The things we say are the things we hear and the things we hear fortify the seeds within us. A clear, scriptural key to maintaining a spirit-filled, faith-activated experience is that of speaking to God, ourselves and others in spiritual songs, concepts of truth, things that are good, pure and lovely.

This is one of the commands for Christians, ***"Speaking to yourselves in psalms and hymns and spiritual songs, singing and making melody in your heart to the Lord;"*** (Ephesians ***5:19.)*** We must also learn to acknowledge with our thoughts all of these things. ***"Casting down imaginations, and every high thing that exalted itself against the knowledge of God, and bringing into captivity every thought to the obedience of Christ,"*** (***2 Corinthians 10:5.)***

One of the conditions of blessing for anyone according to the scriptures is, ***"But his delight and desire are in the law of the Lord, and on His law (the precepts, the instructions, the teachings of God) he habitually meditates (ponders and studies) by day and by night."*** (***Psalms 1:2),*** We should see Christ in the believers around us and think on virtuous things and recognize our place in Christ as kings and priests.

For the Bible say, ***"But you are a chosen generation, a royal priesthood, a dedicated nation, (God's) own purchased, special people, that you may set forth the wonderful deeds and display the virtues and perfections of Him Who called you out of darkness into His marvelous light,"*** (***1 Peter 2:9), a***nd additionally the Scripture confirm, ***"And You have made them a kingdom (royal race) and priests to our God, and they shall reign (as kings)over the earth" (Revelation 5:10.)***

(D.) **Sharing your faith**:

This will inspire your spiritual experience beyond any of the above mentioned safeguarding guides. It is your chance to put your faith into deed! All of the guidelines set forth in this upholding plan will encourage vigour, appeal and steadiness, but witnessing will produce an experience only one of its kind only to itself. The Bible says that there is joy in the presence of God's holy angels when one sinner comes to repentance.

Jesus said, ***"Even so, I tell you, there is joy among and in the presence of the angel of God over one (especially) wicked person who repents (changes his mind for the better, heartily amending his ways, with abhorrence of his past sins)." (Luke 15:10.)*** The joy over one sinner repenting more than over 99 that have already repented might seem unfair, but not so, for each of the 99 has already had such rejoicing over him when he repented. This simply told these hypocrites that it was for sinners that He came and that only one sinner repenting bring joy to heaven. Consequently why all their murmuring over His carrying out His mission on earth!

When you share the gospel with someone and are able to lead him or her to the living water you have found in Christ, it is one of the most exciting, satisfying experiences you will encounter in your walk with Christ. It is the prime objective, the great commission that Christ called us to. ***"And He said to them, Go into the entire world and preach and publish openly the good news (the Gospel) to every creature (of the whole human race)."(Mark 16:15.)***

He said to go out into the highways and by-ways and compel them to come in. ***"And the lord said unto the servant, Go out into the highways and hedges, and compel them to come in, that my house may be filled." (Luke 14:23)*** If we do not, who will? Witnessing or sharing your faith should never be rooted in guilt, but rather in joy, a fervency of the great experience that you have had.

It is simple and easy and the Spirit of the Lord will give you the words to say even though, in your logical mind, you do not think that you would know what to say. Remember, the Bible state that the person that wins soul is wise. ***"The fruit of the righteous is a tree of life; and he that wins souls is wise." (Proverbs 11:30.)*** The righteous produce eternal life for men by winning them to God.

Paulthe Apostle said, ***"As for myself, brethren, when I came to you, I did not come proclaiming to you the testimony and evidence or mystery and secret of God (concerning what He has done through Christ for the salvation of men) in lofty words of eloquent or human philosophy and wisdom: For I resolved to know nothing (to be acquainted with nothing, to make a display of the knowledge of nothing, and to be conscious of nothing) among you except Jesus Christ (the Messiah) and Him crucified.***

And I was in (passed into a state) weakness and fear (dread) and great trembling (after I had come) among you. And my language and my message were not set forth in persuasive (enticing and plausible) words of wisdom, but they were in demonstration of the (Holy) Spirit and power (a proof by the Spirit and power of God, operating on me and stirring in the minds of my hearers the most holy emotions and thus persuading them).So that your faith might not rest in the wisdom of men (human philosophy), but in the power of God." (1 Corinthians 2:1-5).

Chapter 5

CONCERNING JESUS CHRIST

God created all things by Jesus Christ. Not only were all things created by Him, but redemption of creation is by him. All creation came by Jesus Christ through the Holy Spirit, so all redemption comes the same way. It was what Christ did on the cross that made it possible for God to redeem through the power of the Holy Spirit. We earn and deserve nothing; but God gave us all things that pertain to life and godliness, now and hereafter.

"In the beginning (before all time) was the Word (Christ), and the Word was with God, and the Word was God Himself. He was present originally with God. All things were made and came into existence through Him; and without Him was not even one thing made that has come into being. In Him was Life, and the Life was the Light of men. And the Life shines on in the darkness, for the darkness has never overpowered it (put it out or absorbed it or appropriated it, and is unreceptive." John 1:1-4). Not only was the Word with God, but He was God and always will be as much divine as the other two members of the trinity. God created all things by Jesus Christ.

Hear what the Bible say, ***"John answered. A man can receive nothing (he can claim nothing, he can take unto himself nothing) except as it has been granted to him from heaven. (A man must be content to receive the gift which is given him from heaven; there is no other source.) You yourselves are my witnesses (you personally bear me out) that I stated, I am not the Christ (the Anointed One, the Messiah), but I have (only) been sent before Him (in advance of Him, to be His appointed forerunner, His messenger, His announcer).***

He who has the bride is the bridegroom; but the

groomsman who stands by and listens to him rejoices greatly and heartily on account of the bridegroom's voice. This then is my pleasure and joy, and it is now complete. He must increase, but I must decrease. (He must grow more prominent; I must grow less so.) He who comes from above (heaven) is (far) above all (others); he who comes from the earth belongs to the earth, and talks the language of earth (his words are from an earthly stand-point). He who comes from heaven is (far) above all others (far superior to all others in prominence and in excellence).

It is to what He has (actually) seen and heard that He bears testimony, and yet no one accepts His testimony (no one receives His evidence as true). Whoever receives His testimony has set his seal of approval to this: God is true. (That man has definitely certified, acknowledged, declared once and for all, and is himself assured that it is divine truth that God cannot lie). For since He Whom God has sent speaks the words of God (proclaims God's own message), but boundless is the gift God makes of His Spirit!" (John 3:27-34.) It is only in the Lord Jesus Christ that anyone can find eternal life. His name means "Saviour" and anyone who does not believe it and take Him as such cannot be saved.

Apostle Peter talked about taking the unadulterated milk of the Word of God, the pure doctrines of the gospel as recorded in the new covenant as the Bible says ***"For you have been born again. Your new life did not come from your earthly parents because the life they gave you will end in death. But this new life will last forever because it comes from the eternal, living Word of God." (1 Peter 1:23).***

God's Word changes life as long as you abide, remain and continue in Him. If you permit Christ to abide in you, He will remain in you, and if Christ remain in you, then you shall continue in the Son and the Father. Then if you allow Christ to remain in your life, then you will receive eternal life. ***"So you must remain faithful to what you***

have been taught from the beginning: If you do, you will continue to live in fellowship with the son and with the Father. And in this fellowship we enjoy the eternal life He promised us."(1 John 2:24-25).

You must understand that as long as men continue in the Father and in the Son only and as long as they permit such relationship, they will enjoy the eternal life promise. But if they do not permit the Father and Son to abide in their life, then Jesus said, ***"Anyone who part from me is thrown away like a useless branch and withers. Such branches are gathered into a pile to be burned." (John 15:6)*** This is to say that every believer must remain in Him to bring forth fruit. If any man does not abide in Him he is cast forth as a branch and is withered and burned. This is the secret of living in the will of God.

John said, ***"The Father loves the Son and has given (entrusted, committed) everything into His hand. And he who believes in (has faith in, cling to, relies on) the Son has (now possesses) eternal life. But whoever disobeys (is unbelieving toward, refuses to trust in, disregard, is not subject to) the Son will never see (experience) life, but (instead) the wrath of God abides on him. (God's displeasure remains on him; His indignation hangs over him continually.") (John 3: 35-36.)***

Jesus spoke these words, lifted up His eyes to heaven and said, ***"Father, the hour has come. Glorify Your Son, that Your Son also may glorify You, as You have given Him authority over all flesh, that He should give eternal life to as many as You have given Him. And this is eternal life that they may know You, the only true God, and Jesus Christ whom You have sent. I have glorified You on the earth. I have finished the work which You have given Me to do. And now O Father, glorify Me together with Yourself, with the glory which I had with You before the world was." (John 17:1-5.)***

John said, ***"Whoever believes that Jesus is the Christ is born of God, and everyone who loves Him who begot also loves him who is begotten of Him. By this we know***

that we love the children of God, when we love God and keep His commandments. For this is the love of God, that we keep His commandments. And His commandments are not burdensome. For whatever is born of God overcomes the world. And this is the victory that has overcome the world-our faith. Who is he who overcomes the world, but he who believes that Jesus is the Son of God? This is He who came by water and blood-Jesus Christ; not only by water, but by water and blood. And it is the Spirit who bears witness, because the Spirit is truth………..” (1John5:1-21.)

This is what Paul the Apostle said concerning Jesus Christ that, ***“He is the image of the invisible God, the first-born over all creation. For by Him, all things were created that are in heaven and that are on the earth, visible and invisible, whether thrones or dominions or principalities or powers. All things were created through Him and for Him. And He is before all things, and in Him all things consist. And He is the head of the body, the Church, who is the beginning, the first born from the dead, that in all things, He may have preeminence. For it pleased the Father that in Him all the fullness should dwell, and by Him to reconcile all things to Himself, by Him, whether things on earth or things in heaven, having made peace through the blood of His cross.” (Colossians 1:15-20.)***

Listen to what Paul said, ***“Yet indeed I also count all things loss for the excellence of the knowledge of Christ Jesus my Lord, fro whom I have suffered the loss, of all things, and count them as rubbish, that I may gain Christ and be found in Him, not having my own righteousness, which is from the law, but that which is through faith in Christ, the righteousness which is from God by faith; that I may know Him and the power of His resurrection, and the fellowship of His sufferings, being conform to His death, if by any means, I may attain to the resurrection from the dead.” (Philippians 3:8-11.)***

Paul saying is that he not only counts all things a total

loss to win Christ, he depends upon Him to save his own soul. Mans righteousness is not enough but only God's righteousness that comes through Christ Jesus and by faith. Paul wanted to know Christ and the power which was in His resurrection, and to share in His sufferings, even to die as He died.

Everyone will get the result either fleshy or spiritual living; two destinies as Paul, an apostle of the Lord Jesus Christ said, "Do not be deceived, God is not mocked; for whatever a man sows, that he will also reap. For he who sows to his flesh will of the flesh reap corruption; but he who sows to the Spirit will of the Spirit reap everlasting life." (Galatians 6:7-8.)

Just as surely as everything in nature reproduces after its kind, harvests being as sure as the sowings, so every man will reap what he sows and be responsible for his own destiny. It is foolishness to talk about reaping eternal life when one sows to the flesh. It is equal foolishness to talk about being lost if one sows to the Spirit. Nothing avails any thing but a new creation in Christ Jesus. This is the rule of Christianity that redemption is only through Jesus Christ.

Paul said, "***To me, who am less than the least of all the saints, this grace was given that I should preach among Gentiles the unsearchable riches of Christ, and to make all see what is the fellowship of the mystery which from the beginning of the ages has been hidden in God who created all things through Jesus Christ, to the intent that now the manifold wisdom of God might be made known by the church to the principalities and power in the heavenly places, according to the eternal purpose which He accomplished in Christ Jesus our Lord, in whom we have boldness and access with confidence through faith in Him." (Ephesians 3:8-12.)***

The Church a mystery hid in ages past now revealed. God is making the Jews and Gentiles one new body to demonstrate to the principalities and powers in heavenly places the manifold wisdom of God in the eternal purpose.

By the submission of the church to God and Christ and by the manifold wisdom of God to the church the angelic and demon powers, good and evil, are being taught the eternal purpose of God.

The wisdom of God-the gospel of Jesus Christ, which was hidden up to the time of its revelation and which God ordained before this age for us! None of the rulers of this world knew this revelation. If they had known it they would not have crucified the Lord. Prophets searched diligently to understand what they prophesied about it, even angels themselves desired to comprehend it.

Paul mentioned that, ***"But God has revealed them to us through His Spirit. For the Spirit searches all things, yes the deep things of God. For what man know the things of a man except the Spirit of the man which is in him? Even so no one knows the things of God except the Spirit of God. Now we have received, not the Spirit of the world, but the Spirit who is from God, that we might know the things that have been freely given to us by God."(1 Corinthians 2:10-12.)***

You must understand that human wisdom and preaching of the cross are opposite. The preaching of Christ, the gospel, and the cross is God's power to save the souls of men. ***"For the message of the cross is foolishness to those who are perishing, but to us who are being saved, it is the power of God. For it is written: "I will destroy the wisdom of the wise, and bring to nothing the understanding of the prudent." (1 Corinthians 1:18-19.)***

These are the things God has chosen and the reasons are:

(1.) Foolish things to confound the wise.

(2.) Weak things to confound mighty.

(3.) Base things to humble the exalted.

(4.) Despised things to humble noble.

(5.) Powerless things to bring to defeat the things that are powerful.

Chapter 6

Three Steps to Calvary: Death, Burial and Resurrection.

May I remind you that, there were three steps to Calvary: death, burial, and resurrection. The way to accept Calvary in our individual life is to accept the death, burial, and resurrection of Christ. We don't have to literally die, be buried, and rise again. Jesus was our substitute and did this for us. All we must do is accept what He did by spiritually dying, symbolically being buried, and spiritually rising again.

Repentance:

We take on His death by repentance, which is spiritual death. When a person truly repents, he dies out to his own will, renounces it forever, and vows to live from that time on according to the will of Jesus Christ.

Baptism:

We take on His burial by baptism in water, by immersion into His name. Romans 6:4 says, "Therefore we are buried with him by baptism". Baptism must be done by immersion; for something cannot be buried by sprinkling a little dirt on top of it. That burial, after a few days, would certainly prove to be insufficient! Furthermore, every baptism of which we have biblical record was administered by immersion. That alone should determine our course of action on this matter.

Infilling of the Holy Spirit:

Finally, we partake of the resurrection of Jesus Christ by

the infilling of the Holy Ghost. This is the new life that enables us to live as a Christian should. We see then that Being Born Again means to spiritually die—repent; symbolically be buried—baptism; and spiritually rise again—receive the Holy Ghost. Thus, in plain language an individual must repent of his sins, be baptized in the name of Jesus Christ by immersion, and receive the gift of the Holy Ghost.

The Bible says, "And there are three that bear witness in the earth, the Spirit, and the water, and the blood: and these three agree in one."(1 John 5:8). What is the one thing in which the spirit, water, and blood agree? Is it not the new birth? Blood covers our sins at repentance; the waters of baptism wash them away, thus making us clean for the Spirit to come into our lives to dwell.

When the Roman soldiers thrust the spear into Jesus' side after He died, the scripture tells us that there came forth blood and water (John 19:34). This was for cleansing of the nations. It takes blood and water to eradicate sin. Blood is the cleansing agent, and water is the flushing agent. When a jar is washed for canning, soap AND water are necessary to cleanse that jar so that it might be filled with good fruit.

Likewise, blood and water are necessary to cleanse the human soul so that it may receive the Spirit of Christ, which is the Holy Ghost. This teaching was verified by Peter when he said, "Repent and be baptized for the remission of sins" (Acts 2:38). Repentance and baptism are both absolutely essential for the remission of sins!

Paul taught that the three steps of Calvary is the gospel that we should preach. "Moreover, brethren, I declare unto you the gospel which I preached unto you, which also ye have received, and wherein ye stand; By which also ye are saved, if ye keep in memory what I have preached unto you, unless ye have believed in vain. For I delivered unto you first of all that which I also received, how that Christ died for our sins according to the scriptures; And that he was buried, and that he rose again the third day according to the scriptures." (1 Corinthians 15:1-4).

Paul went on to say in II Thessalonians 1:7-8, "And to you who are troubled rest with us, when the Lord Jesus shall be revealed from heaven with his mighty angels, In flaming fire taking vengeance on them that know not God, and that obey not the gospel of our Lord Jesus Christ." Paul told us that the gospel is the death, burial, and resurrection of Christ. How can we obey the death, burial, and resurrection?

We obey by repentance, baptism, and receiving the Holy Ghost as we have previously explained. Notice that the Lord Jesus is to appear "in flaming fire taking vengeance on them that know not God, and that obey not the gospel." It is absolutely necessary for every human being to obey the gospel by being born again. Jesus told Nicodemus, "Ye must be born again." (John 3:7).

Chapter 7

The Old Testament Speaks of the Being Born Again Plan.

May I share with you another Biblical lesson given to us concerning this subject. The Bible teaches us that the things of the Old Testament were types and shadows of the things to come. When the priests of the law ministered by offering sacrifices, there were three major steps to their duties.

I want you to picture this, first they slew the animal to be offered on the brazen altar. The blood here was shed and caught into a container for use in the Holy Place. The flesh of the animal was to be consumed by fire. This teaches us the first step of salvation—repentance. When we repent, we present our bodies a living sacrifice, and our sins are covered by the blood of Jesus.

After the shedding of blood, the priests were ordered to wash at the laver and to cleanse themselves with water in preparation for entering the Holy Place. The laver, a round fountain-like structure, was overlaid in the bottom with a looking glass. When the priest bent over to wash, he was able to see himself so that he could be sure that he was clean. When an individual is baptized, he should examine himself to be sure that he is leaving the world behind once and for all.

We see then that the second step of the tabernacle ministry plainly teaches us of water baptism. Blood and water were used to cleanse and prepare them for entry into the Holy Place, even as blood and water cleanses us in preparation of receiving the Holy One into our lives!

After cleansing, the priest would take the fire from the brazen altar and enter through the veil into the Holy Place. The Holy Place had no doors or windows through which light could come. The only light would come from the golden candlesticks. These candlesticks consisted of seven wicks fed by oil from seven bowls. The wicks had to be lit with the fire brought by the priest from the brazen altar.

The uniting of the oil and fire at the candlesticks to produce light is a perfect type of the Holy Ghost and fire promised to New Testament believers (Matthew 3:11). Without the light of the Holy Ghost we could not see to live in the Holy Place, which is where every Christian should live.

God spoke of His great plan of redemption in the Old Testament in types and shadows; and then in the New Testament He spoke plainly to us so that we would have no doubt of His will! "There are three that bear witness in the earth, the spirit, the water, and the blood; and these three agree in one." (1 John 5:8). I believe that this Old Testament lesson beautifully reaffirms to us the absolute necessity of the full Born Again plan in each life for salvation!

Chapter 8

Common Misconceptions About Salvation

Believe on the Lord Jesus Christ:

Hear what the Scripture say, “Sirs, what must I do to be saved? And they said, Believe on the Lord Jesus Christ, and thou shalt be saved, and thy house.” (Acts 16: 30-31). Many have taken this scripture to teach that all that is required for salvation is to believe that Jesus Christ is the Saviour of the world; and from that point on the individual is saved. It is definitely true that an individual must believe that Jesus is the Saviour in order to be saved.

However, Paul, who spoke these words in Acts 16, has some further teaching on the subject that says, “For whosoever shall call upon the name of the Lord shall be saved. How then shall they call on him of whom they have not heard? and how shall they hear without a preacher? And how shall they preach, except they be sent?” (Romans 10: 13-15).

If we wanted to be absurd, we could take this thirteenth verse to teach that all an individual must do for salvation is to call out the name of Jesus one time and he has received salvation. Paul tells us they can’t call on him in whom they have not believed.

Furthermore, he said that they couldn’t believe in him of whom they have not heard. We cannot merely believe. We must believe something about Christ. When Paul told the jailer in Acts 16 to believe on the Lord Jesus Christ, he went on to speak unto him the word of the Lord (verse 32). The word which Paul spoke was apparently the gospel; for the result in verse 33 was that the jailer and all his house were baptized at midnight. That’s how essential baptism is for salvation. Paul took all these people out at midnight and baptized them!

Some would object here by saying that we are saved by faith alone. It is true that we are saved by faith, but it is also true that true faith always produces action on the part of the believer. Let's study from James 2:14-22 to verify this point.

The Bible say, "What doth it profit, my brethren, though a man say he hath faith, and have not works? can faith save him? If a brother or a sister be naked, and destitute of daily food, And one of you say unto them, Depart in peace, be ye warmed and filled; notwithstanding ye give them not those things which are needful to the body; what doth it profit? Even so faith if it hath not works, is dead, being alone.

Yea, a man may say, Thou hast faith, and I have works; shew me thy faith without thy works, and I will shew thee my faith by my works. Thou believest that there is one God; thou doest well: the devils also believe, and tremble. But wilt thou know, O vain man, that faith without works is dead? Was not Abraham our father justified by works when he had offered Isaac his son upon the altar? Seest thus how faith wrought with his works, and by works was faith made perfect?" (James 2: 14-22).

When an individual believes on the Lord Jesus Christ, what do they believe about Him? They believe the gospel, which is the death, burial, and resurrection (I Corinthians 15:1-4). James teaches us that faith without action is dead, or it is not really faith at all. When a sinner hears the true gospel and truly believes, he will obey the gospel.

An individual obeys the death, burial, and resurrection of Christ by repentance, baptism in Jesus' name, and the infilling of the Holy Ghost, evidenced by speaking with other tongues. This is the salvation of Calvary!

May I say that, if you are still having trouble conceding to this teaching because of the element of works involved, let's reason concerning one more point. Being Born Again, — Repentance, Baptism, and receiving the Holy Ghost is not considered by God to be a work.

The Bible mentioned that, "Not by works of

righteousness which we have done, but according to his mercy he saved us, by the washing of regeneration, and the renewing of the Holy Ghost" (Titus 3:5). This book is written for you to understand that Regeneration, which is Being Born Again, is not a work of righteousness.

In conclusion to this matter, let me cite a familiar Biblical example. In the great revival at Samaria in Acts 8:5-23, a sorcerer named Simon heard the preaching of Philip. He believed and was baptized and continued with Philip beholding the signs and miracles that were done. Many people would say that because Simon believed, he was saved.

Yet the Apostle Peter said of him that, "For I perceive that thou art in the gall of bitterness, and in the bond of iniquity." (Acts 8:23). I can say to you with this example from the Scripture that it is impossible for anyone in the bond of iniquity to be saved; for the scriptures tell us, "If the Son therefore shall make you free, ye shall be free indeed" (John 8:36). Simon believed and was baptized, but he had not received the Holy Ghost; therefore, he was not born again.

Truth be told, We cannot be half-born and survive. The entire work of Calvary is necessary for our salvation.

DECISION TIME

May I encourage you to accept Jesus Christ as your personal Lord and Saviour today! The Bible say, "***Because if you acknowledge and confess with your lips that Jesus is Lord and in your heart believe (adhere to, trust in, and rely on the truth) that God raised Him from the dead, you will be saved. For with the heart a person believes (adhere to, trusts in, and relies on Christ) and so is justified (declared righteous, acceptable to God), and with the mouth he confesses (declares openly and speaks out freely his faith) and confirms (his) salvation." (Romans 10:9-10.)***

Pray this Prayer with me!

"Lord Jesus, I believe that you died for me and rose again on the third day. I confess that I am a sinner that needs your love and forgiveness. Come into my heart, forgive my sins. I receive your eternal life and confirm your love by giving me peace, joy and supernatural love for other people, in Jesus mighty name" Amen.

OTHER BOOKS BY:

Charles O. Soyoye

Marriage, a Miracle of Completion
The Secret of Living in the Will of God

Available from your local bookstore!

www.ingramcontent.com/pod-product-compliance
Ingram Content Group UK Ltd.
Pitfield, Milton Keynes, MK11 3LW, UK
UKHW042000190726
13854UKWH00005B/2089

9 781785 077104